# THE GREATER
## WORDS OF POWER

THE SECRET CALLS OF ARCHANGEL MAGICK

DAMON BRAND

THE GALLERY OF
MAGICK

Copyright © 2016 Damon Brand

All Rights Reserved. This book may not be reproduced, in whole or in part, in any form or by any means electronic or mechanical, including photocopying, recording, or by any information storage retrieval system now known or hereafter invented, without written permission from the publisher, The Gallery of Magick.

*It is hereby expressly stated that the images in this book may not be reproduced in any form, except for individual and personal use. Derivative works based on these images or the associated concepts are not permitted, and any such attempt to create a derivative work will be met with legal action.*

Disclaimer: Consider all information in this book to be speculation and not professional advice, to be used at your own risk. Damon Brand and The Gallery of Magick are not responsible for the consequences of your actions. Success depends on the integrity of your workings, the initial conditions of your life and your natural abilities, so results will vary. The information is never intended to replace or substitute for financial advice from a professional advisor, and when it comes to matters of finance you should always seek conventional, professional advice. The information is provided on the understanding that you will use it in accordance with the laws of your country.

# CONTENTS

| | |
|---|---|
| The Magick of Words | 7 |
| Speaking the Words of Power | 11 |
| How to Use the Greater Words of Power | 15 |
| The Art of Magick | 20 |
| Adapting the Method | 23 |
| The Activation Ritual | 26 |
| The Greater Words of Power | 31 |

## Rituals of the Mind — 33
| | |
|---|---|
| Increase Self Confidence | 34 |
| Complete a Task | 36 |
| Increase Energy Levels | 38 |
| Pass an Exam | 40 |
| Mental Focus | 42 |
| Obtain Peaceful Sleep and Dreams | 44 |
| Overcome Bad Habits | 46 |
| Increase Willpower to Eat Well | 48 |

## Rituals That Affect Others — 51
| | |
|---|---|
| Stop an Argument Quickly | 52 |
| Receive a Fair Legal Decision | 54 |
| Subdue Unwanted Attention | 56 |
| Give Comfort to Another | 58 |
| Make People Warmer Toward You | 60 |
| Encourage Change | 62 |

## Rituals of Emotion — 65
| | |
|---|---|
| Make New Friends | 66 |
| Attract a Romantic Partner | 68 |
| End a Relationship Easily | 70 |
| Banish Fear and Worry | 72 |
| Improve Your Mood | 74 |
| Improve the Mood of Those Around You | 76 |
| Recover Lost Love | 78 |

## Rituals of Creativity — 81
| | |
|---|---|
| Enhance Creativity | 82 |
| Become Popular for Your Creative Work | 84 |
| Improve Visual Skills | 86 |
| Improve Musical Abilities | 88 |

| | |
|---|---|
| **Rituals of Transformation** | **91** |
| The Road Opener | 92 |
| Recover Your Passion | 94 |
| Overcome Lost Love | 96 |
| Increase Psychic Connection | 98 |
| Overcome Bitterness, Jealousy and Hatred | 100 |
| Receive Guidance | 102 |
| When Magick Works | 105 |
| Appendix A: What the Words Mean | 107 |

# The Magick of Words

The secret word combinations in this book can connect you to divine power, through the magick of angels and archangels.

When your need is real, speak these words and you bring the magick to life. The ritual process is extremely simple, and yet the rewards can be great. The magick is aimed at getting direct results that improve your life.

You may be relieved to discover how straightforward the process is, when compared to other magickal systems, but do not underestimate the power of these words. The first book on this subject, *Words of Power,* has led to thousands of people discovering magick, with a system that is often described as being deceptively simple. That same system is presented here, but this book introduces thirty-one new magickal powers.

The magick in this book will give you the power to obtain mental focus, overcome procrastination, pass exams, increase energy, sleep peacefully, overcome bad habits and increase the willpower to eat well.

There is magick of influence that can stop arguments quickly, ensure fair legal decisions, subdue unwanted attention, make people warmer to you, and encourage those who are stuck in their ways to change.

With the rituals of emotion, you will be able to encourage new friendship, attract a romantic partner, end a relationship easily, banish fear and worry, improve your mood and the mood of those around you, or recover lost love.

There is magick to enhance creativity, and to make your creative work well liked, as well as improving artistic skills and musical ability.

One of the most powerful rituals is *The Road Opener*, which can help you discover new pathways, and new directions in life that can be truly rewarding. Other rituals of transformation help you recover your passion, overcome lost love, increase your psychic connection to another, overcome bitterness, jealousy and hatred, and receive angelic guidance.

This book is described as 'greater' because every ritual gives you a direct connection to archangel magick. By naming sacred aspects of the archangels, and the angel messengers that answer directly to these archangels, your desire is made clear to the most potent and powerful spiritual beings. When you convey your need, the angels respond, and the archangels reward your request with a result.

I also feel the book is worthy of the title 'greater' because the specific rituals revealed here work on an extremely deep level, changing your life in accordance with the authentic desire that lies beneath your surface desire. You only need to focus on what you want, and the magick will give you what is most likely to work for you, and what can bring you satisfaction. You get the results you ask for, and they come to you in ways that are harmonious and in keeping with your needs.

You don't need to have faith, to believe in anything, or use will power. To get this magick to work, you only need to learn a few simple magickal techniques. You don't need to fast, pray, cleanse, cast a circle, use a wand or burn incense. This magick is directed by your heart, so you need nothing other than this book and your own desire for change.

If you're completely new to magick, this book can get you started. If you've been using magick for decades, this is an excellent shortcut to magickal success.

Please read the book thoroughly, to understand the process. Although this magick is simple when compared to other ritual methods, you should take the time to fully understand the method before attempting the magick. To get results, make sure you read all the chapters, because the background information is a vital key that helps unlock the magick.

If you've already used the original *Words of Power*, the method covered here is almost identical, and the bulk of the text is not going to be altogether revolutionary for you. What counts is that you get thirty-one new sigils and calls, which can be used to change your life in completely new ways. You may want to read the instructions in the following chapters, and use the modified activation process, for the sake of completion. It's almost identical to what you've done before.

If you've never read *Words of Power*, that's also completely fine. *The Greater Words of Power* is a self-contained system, and everything you need is here. It offers a unique range of magickal powers.

The secret word combinations in this book were discovered by The Gallery of Magick. We are a group of seventeen occultists, and we have been refining magick for the last few decades. The word combinations in this book represent the most streamlined magick we have ever discovered.

If you feel skeptical, that's fine, and I can only urge you to experience the magick for yourself. There are countless stories of this magick working, but nothing teaches so well as experience. When you feel the magick working for you, you will know its true potential.

When you speak these words, you are using divine names and angelic names. Some of these are well known within occult circles and some are more obscure. It is the combination of these words, along with the magickal technique of emotional transmutation (described later in the book), that makes this magick so effective.

A word may, for example, be a name that links to specific powers of a mighty archangel, without naming the archangel directly. You scan over the words with your eyes and vocalize the sounds. By viewing the letters, and calling these words and names, in the order shown, you are able to convey your desire to the angels. This is the essential technique. The angels will understand your need, and it is their sacred duty to respond when called.

The magick is safe, because each ritual contains words that enshrine the working with divine protection and power.

You will notice that the sigils in this book contain the

words written in Hebrew, but you do not need to be able to read Hebrew. This magick works for people from all religions that we know about, so there is no need for a Western or Judeo-Christian background. The Hebrew is a shortcut that helps you access the angels. Beneath each sigil, the words are all spelt phonetically, so saying them is easy.

The sigils contain a visual device of a pentagram, split into a light and dark section. This image can help to make your reality more open to change. Also, because this device is used in the activation sigil, it lets your subconscious mind know when you are working with the Words of Power. If you have any fear regarding the pentagram, please read about its sacred history (there's a reasonable entry on Wikipedia), and know it has nothing to do with evil.

If you are new to magick, you may have heard that some form of payment or sacrifice is required in order to receive results. Some people fear that when they perform magick, the magick will bite back and take a fee, if no sacrifice has been made. These fears are based on superstition and rumors regarding very particular styles of magick. The magick of *The Greater Words of Power* does not require you to pay the angels with anything other than gratitude for the result you receive.

Magick can give you what you ask for, so make sure that you ask for the things you truly desire. Perform the magick with great confidence, knowing that it is safe.

## Speaking the Words of Power

When you first see the Words of Power, you may wonder whether you'll be able to say them correctly. You can trust me when I say that this book is absolutely Pronunciation Proof. Because you scan the letters visually, you don't need to get the pronunciation perfectly correct.

You should know that the pronunciations in this book are not always objectively correct, but we have found many pronunciations that work easily for western speakers, and that produce the desired effect. That is what you find here. If you have any problems, there's a video on The Gallery of Magick website (**www.galleryofmagick.com**) that lets you hear how this all works.

Speak the words in capitals as though they are English. So, you may see a word such as this:

AH-DEER-EAR-AWN

This is one word, made up from four different sounds. You read the sounds as though they are English. That would be as follows:

**AH**. The first sound is just the word *ah*.

**DEER** is the word *deer*.

**EAR** is the word *ear*.

**AWN** is like *lawn* without the l.

Run these together and you get AH-DEER-EAR-AWN.

As you can see, it is quite easy to work out how to say the sounds, by finding an English equivalent.

If you see the sound UB, you know it sounds the same as *rub* without the *r*. If you see RAWG, you know this is the word *raw* with the *g* sound added at the end. It's very easy and takes just a few minutes to learn the words for each ritual.

It's worth looking at some of the more commonly used sounds in this book. If these are even close to being correct, you'll be doing a great job.

## UH

**UH** is *up* without the *p*. So, if you see the sound **KUH**, you know that it sounds like *cup* without the *p*.

## AH

The **AH** sound is like the *ah* you get in *ma* and *pa*. When you say *ma* without the *m*, you've got the right sound.

## EH

**EH** is like the middle part of the word *net*. Say *net* without the *n* or the *t* and you've got **EH**.

## AW

**AW** is like *awe*, or *raw* without the *r*. So if you see **KAWV**, you know it sounds like the word *awe* with *k* at the beginning and *v* at the end.

## AY

**AY** is like *pay* without the *p*. So if you see **NAY**, it's like *pay* with *n* instead of *p*.

## G

**G** sounds like the *g* in *give*, rather than the *g* in *gem*. So **GAH** sounds like the first part of *garlic*, (before you get to the *r*).

## TZ

**TZ** is like the end of the word *cats*. If you spell it as *catz*, that's even better.

## CH

Authentic Hebrew often uses the *ch* sound that you hear in the Scottish word *loch*, or the German *achtung*. Our video shows the sound you want to get. Alternatively, you can simply make a **K** sound when you see **CH**.

To illustrate this, you will soon see the word **CHUH**. This is the **CH** sound described above, followed by **UH**. If you can't make the guttural *ch* sound, then replace it with a *k*. So **CHUH** becomes **KUH**, and sounds like *uh* with a *k* at the front.

This may seem complicated, but remember that for the most part, you are reading English sounds, and if you remain relaxed about it, you will have access to powerful magick.

The only real challenge is **CH,** and even that doesn't have to be perfect. You can try for the correct sounding **CH**, or just sound it as **K** instead. The book *is* Pronunciation Proof and will work if you say the words with the emotional transmutation described in the next chapter.

It is perfectly safe to practice the words before you actually come to perform the ritual, and I would recommend that you take the time to do this, so you can feel relaxed about the ritual itself.

If you've already worked with *Words of Power*, you'll see that some words appear in both books, but are pronounced differently here. This is intentional, and you don't need to change how you work with the other book.

## How to Use the Greater Words of Power

You don't need any equipment, other than this book. What you do need is an open mind, and a willingness to work with your emotions. Central to this magick is a process known as emotional transmutation. When you perform a ritual you notice how you feel about the situation as it stands, and then imagine how good you will feel when the magick works. This process is extremely simple, but cannot be excluded from the magick.

Before you begin the magick proper, you will need to work the activation ritual in a subsequent chapter. That ritual connects you to the Words of Power, and to the imagery of the sigils. Take the time to perform that activation ritual, and then when you are ready, choose the ritual that is appropriate for your needs. When you have chosen your ritual, do this:

### Contemplate the change

Sit in a quiet place, and contemplate the problem, challenge or aspect of your life that you want to change. Notice how the problem makes you feel. At this point, you are not trying to find a solution or imagine how things could change. Feel the pain, discomfort or other emotions that surround the issue. Your feelings do not have to be strong, but notice how you feel when you think about the target of your magick.

If, for example, you want to use *The Road Opener*, it is probably because your life feels blocked. That may make you feel tired, angry, frustrated, or it may just give you a vaguely negative feeling. Whatever you feel is valid, so *feel* it.

This process only needs to take about a minute.

### Scan the sigil

Scan each word in the sigil, looking at the letter shapes from right to left. This is the opposite way to reading standard

English, because Hebrew is read from right to left. Start with the uppermost word and work your way down the list. You do not need to do anything other than see the word. You're not reading but *scanning* the letters. You're letting them sink into your consciousness, and that is enough.

This is what one word looks like, and you scan it from right to left, as shown by the arrow.

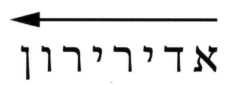

You let your eyes settle on each letter, but you don't have to stare. The entire scan of a word won't take more than a few seconds, at most.

During this visual scan you may feel the negative emotions from earlier. That is OK. If the emotion fades away, that is also fine. For this part of the process, keep your focus on scanning the letters and letting them become a part of you.

### Experience the solution

Imagine the relief and gratitude you would feel if your problem was solved. This transmutes your emotion from the negative emotion you felt earlier, to match the positive emotion you want to achieve. It also helps if you allow a feeling of gratitude to mingle into your emotions.

So, if the magick worked, how would you feel? That's all you have to imagine. And imagine it *as though it's already happened*. You might feel elated, calm, joyous or something else subtler and more abstract. Let yourself feel the emotion, as though you have the result right now. And feel grateful that you feel so good.

Do not concern yourself with how the result might be achieved. Do not try to think about the steps required for the problem to be solved. If you're looking to *Improve Musical Abilities,* you don't need to think about the steps you'll take. Not yet. You just imagine how good it would feel to master a new musical skill, for example. Your focus should be on the result you want, not how you get there.

In terms of results, you can be general or specific. You may want a general improvement in your understanding of melody, or you may want to learn a particular musical scale. Be general if you want a general improvement, and be specific if you want to direct the magick. But don't worry about how this manifestation will come about. Focus only on the emotion of the result, and how you will feel when the magick works.

The feeling does not have to be incredibly intense or clear. Just catch a hint of the feeling, and the transmutation will empower your magick.

Once you have that feeling, speak the Words of Power.

### Speak the words

Continue to feel the emotion, and now speak the Words of Power. They are printed beneath the sigil. There is one complete word on each line. Each word is made of several sounds. So YEE-KAH-HAH-RAW-VUH-HAH is a single word.

These are read as though they are English, from left to right. Read each word, just once, and as you say the word, feel the emotion of your desired result. Then move to the next word on the next line. If the emotion fades slightly as you continue, that's OK, but try to maintain a feeling of gratitude, as though the magick has already worked.

Between each word, glance up at the sigil. You do not need to look at a particular word, but simply glance at the sigil for a moment, and then speak the next word.

If you are alone and can say the words loudly, then let the words vibrate through your throat. It's as though you are breathing the words out, letting them rumble up from your belly through the back of your throat. It's almost as though you are chanting or singing them.

This 'vibration', where you let the words rumble out of you is not essential, and will be impossible for many, so if need be, just say them out loud.

How you say the words is less important than the feeling you have when you speak. Remember that every word is a divine name, or a connection to a spirit that works the will of the divine. Each time you say a word, speak *as though you are being heard by the spirits*.

You are charging the spirits to do your bidding, but it's important to say the words *to* somebody. Imagine what happens when you call your friend's name. You are not simply saying a word; you are calling a name *to* your friend. The same should be true of every Word of Power. Make it feel as though you are sending your emotion out with each word you call. You are not talking to yourself, but communicating your emotion to angelic beings.

If you need to perform your magick in silence, for the sake of privacy or any other reason, you can do so. Some people whisper the words, and others simply say them in their heads. Either method works so long as you imagine you are calling the names to the ends of the universe. This is one reason why silence can actually be better than whispering, because you can imagine that you're calling the words out to eternity, but if you whisper, it can make the words seem quiet and small. Choose a method that you're comfortable with and it will work.

### Let go of the result

When the magick is over, it is over, and it is your job to let the magick work. You do this by trusting it. If you don't actually trust it or believe in it, you can act *as though* you trust it by taking your attention off the magick. Just assume you'll get what you asked for.

If you keep checking whether or not the magick has worked, or counting how many hours and days have passed since your ritual, you are lusting for result. This lust is the opposite of trust. Take your attention off the magick, and the magick will work better than when you pester it with anxious thoughts and impatience. If you find yourself thinking about the result you want, you don't have to banish it from your mind; let yourself feel pleasure, as though the result has already come about. This helps you avoid lust for result.

You should also do your part to encourage the change to take place. If you're using magick to attract a romantic partner, or make new friends, do what you can to attend social gatherings. Don't sit at home and hope that the magick will do everything. It can work near-miracles, but when you put in a small effort, the magick magnifies your effort more than you might imagine possible.

With some rituals, it's very clear how you can do your part. If you're using magick to pass an exam, you should prepare well. That's common sense. But for some rituals, such as *Increase Self Confidence*, you may wonder what you can actually do. Remain open to the magick working, and also be on the lookout for situations where you feel an urge to get comfortable with your new skill or state of mind. These opportunities will almost certainly arise.

It's important to respond to coincidence. When magick works, you will find that it often does so through a string of coincidences. You won't notice them all, but when you do notice coincidence, respond by accepting the offer of the coincidence. That is, recognize the magick, rather than just going, 'Oh, what a strange coincidence.'

So if you try to attract a new romantic partner, and that day you are invited to a social event that you would never normally go to, you should go. If you're using magick to improve your musical skills, and you happen to meet a really good music instructor, don't write that off as mere coincidence. It is *magickal coincidence*. And it may be exactly what you need to get the result you want.

Magickal results occur in ways that you might not expect, and when you least expect them. When a magickal result does arise, feel grateful that you got what you wanted, even if it occurred with a slight twist. The more gratitude you feel for results that do come, the better magick works for you in the future. You do not need to call out to the angels to thank them, but make sure that you enjoy the result, and feel grateful. The angels will know.

Magick can manifest in so many ways. If you do magick to improve your musical skills, you may just get better as you practice, without any new teacher appearing in your life. If you do magick to make people warmer toward you, people may change overnight. These results feel truly magickal. But don't dismiss the results that come through more ordinary channels. If mundane reality seems to give you the result you want, know that mundane reality was shaped by high magick.

Also, be wary of writing off a result as a failure, just because it didn't manifest when you wanted it to. If you truly let go, and accept that the magick will work when the time is right, then the right time may come very soon. But if you say, 'That ritual didn't work,' through impatience, you stifle the magick. Leave your rituals open, and be grateful when the results come. Bear in mind that results can come to you instantly, or they can take three hours, three days, three weeks, three months or more. Most of the time, people find this magick works exceptionally fast. If it does, accept the result with gratitude, but if it doesn't come as quickly as you want, know that patience will bring you the rewards you seek.

### The Art of Magick

It can be tempting to use several rituals on one problem, but you may find that a single well-chosen ritual is more effective.

More magick doesn't always make for faster or better results. One ritual, performed with great focus, will often be more effective than several rituals.

There is no theoretical limit regarding how much magick you can perform, and there is nothing to stop you using every ritual in the book. You may find, however, that leaving some time between rituals makes it easier for you to generate the required focus. Whether that means leaving an hour, a day or a week between rituals is down to your personal experience of the magick, and how easy you find it to perform.

You only need to perform a ritual once, for any given situation. Let's say you're using the first ritual in the book, to *Increase Self Confidence*. You perform this ritual just once. If you feel you didn't quite get it right, you are free to repeat it at a later time, but there is usually no need, and you get good results when you perform the magick just once, with confidence.

You can also repeat a ritual when circumstances change. If you find that certain events, situations or habits of thought lead you to lose your confidence, or if you find you need more confidence than ever, you can repeat that ritual. But if there's no actual change in circumstances, there's no need to repeat the ritual. So if you are working to *Recover Your Passion*, don't think that working the ritual every day is going to make the magick work faster and better. Perform the ritual once, and let it work in its own time. Only repeat it should something happen to make your passion fall away once more.

You may find that some rituals need to be repeated every few weeks, as circumstances change. But only feel the need to repeat the magick *when* the circumstances change. Otherwise, you can perform a ritual just once.

If you use the ritual to *Stop an Argument Quickly*, and two hours later there's a new argument, then of course you can repeat the magick. You will find that in most cases, the magick continues to work for some time.

There is no harm in repeating rituals, so why do I emphasize that once is usually enough? Partly to stop you repeating rituals out of lust for result, and also to save time. When you start your car, you don't keep turning the key after the engine has fired. The same applies here. With this magick, know that the work is done, and you only have to allow yourself to receive the desired results. Patience brings fast results. If your life changes, and you need to use a ritual again, there is no harm in that at all.

Often, you will find that you can solve a problem by choosing the right ritual, performing it and letting the results come when they come. Sometimes, though, if a problem feels more complicated, you may feel the need to use multiple rituals.

Let's imagine that you're trying to pass an exam. You could use the *Pass an Exam* ritual while you are learning, and *Mental Focus* on the day of the exam. You might also feel that your nerves affect you, and so use magick to *Increase Self Confidence*, and *Increase Energy Levels* to ensure you get through the big day. This approach is wise, but don't use more than one ritual if you don't need it. If you actually have sufficient energy and confidence, don't assume that adding these rituals in will increase your chances of success. This magick responds to genuine needs, so keep your focus on areas that you are certain you want to change. You might only need to use the *Mental Focus* ritual on the day of the exam. If so, keep it as simple as that.

Magick can be highly energizing, but some people find it can also leave you a little drowsy for a few minutes. Bear this in mind when timing your rituals, and give yourself enough time to come back to reality when the ritual is complete. Most people find the magick actually increases personal energy, so even if you feel relaxed, you might feel a bit sharper than before, and you may perceive the world with slightly more depth, color and beauty.

## Adapting the Method

I have emphasized the importance of patience, but there is a way of adapting this method so it can be used at great speed, when your need is urgent. You can also adapt the basic method so that you can work the magick for other people.

To use the magick at great speed, you will need to put in some preparation, and learn two words. With a little effort, you have powerful magick at your disposal.

Let's imagine that you want the ability to *Stop an Argument Quickly*, but no argument is currently underway. There may be an angry person in your life, and you want to have the magick to hand, but you know that when an argument erupts you won't have the opportunity to go and perform the ritual. So here's what you do.

Perform the ritual, and keep the emotions general. Do not imagine a specific argument or person. Begin the ritual by focusing on how powerless or upset arguments make you feel, and then before you read the words, imagine how good it would be to be able to stop arguments. Even though this is quite abstract, you should still be able to generate the required emotions. Complete the ritual using these emotions.

Now you need to take note of the first word and the last word from your chosen ritual. In this case, those words are AH-DEER-EAR-AWN and REE-YEE. When you need to use the magick in an emergency situation, you only need to say these two words, and the entire ritual will be activated.

When the need arises say the words, out loud if you can, and remember that your request is being heard by the spirits you are calling on.

This emergency version of the magick does not work for everything. You will probably never have need to use an emergency version of *Increase Willpower to Eat Well*, as that requires ongoing attention rather than a quick fix. But you can make great use of many rituals, by preparing them for future use. All you need is the ability to remember the first and last words of your chosen ritual. If your memory is excellent, you can prepare several of these. Otherwise, learn only those that you need the most.

Remember, you must perform the full ritual as preparation. Using the two words alone, without this preparation, will not produce results.

To perform the magick for others, first consider whether the other person wants the magick to be performed. It is acceptable to work magick without consent, and often it can work more readily if the target of your magick is unaware, because this avoids them lusting for result. Make sure, however, that you have done everything you can to ascertain that the person truly wants something to change. We often assume we know what people want, but what they really want remains hidden.

If you feel confident that helping somebody else would be the right thing to do, then simply perform the ritual, but imagine that you are the other person. In the first part of the ritual, imagine the other person's negative feelings, and actually feel those emotions. Then imagine that you (as the other person), obtain the result you want. Feel the relief and gratitude as though you are the other person, while performing the remainder of the ritual.

If that approach is beyond your imaginative abilities, there is an alternative process. Simply perform the ritual, knowing that you want to change the situation for the other person, and focus on *your own* feelings regarding the problem.

If you know somebody who is suffering from agonizing writer's block, for example, you might use the *Enhance Creativity* ritual. At the outset you imagine how *you* feel about the other person's difficulty. You may feel tired of hearing complaints, or you may be truly empathetic or just frustrated. Whatever you honestly feel, *feel it*. Then when you transmute the emotion in the second part of the ritual, imagine how *you* will feel when the other person's creativity improves. You may feel proud, relieved, happy, elated. Whatever you would feel, *feel it*, and also feel grateful that the magick has worked.

The core of this book involves using the magick patiently, to change aspects of your own life, but if you feel in tune with the magick, you will find that it responds well to these adaptations.

## The Activation Ritual

Before you first use *The Greater Words of Power*, you need to attune yourself to the sigils in this book. By using the following ritual, you activate your connection to the sigils. The short time it takes to complete this ritual will set you up for life.

The activation ritual only needs to be performed once, ever. If you take the time to read the instructions, and learn the sounds of the words before you begin, you will find this quite easy. Do not let the simplicity make you think this is trivial or unnecessary. It is a key to the magick in this book.

Some people worry that they have not done a good enough job with this ritual. If so, you are free to repeat it, but please note that repeating this will not make the magick stronger. Use it once, and know that you are being attuned to the sigils in this book.

This ritual does not activate the words, so much as it activates your connection to them. The two activation sigils that appear on the following pages contain Words of Power that help establish this connection. Also, this is your introduction to the visual device of the two-tone pentagram. By using these two sigils, you come to experience this visual device as a gateway to magick.

In practice, all you need to do is follow these brief instructions.

Gaze at the first sigil for about a minute. You are not trying to think or feel anything specific, but you can allow yourself to become peaceful as you gaze.

Starting at the top of the sigil, scan over each word, from right to left, as described earlier. You are not reading, or attempting to understand, but simply letting the shape of the Hebrew letters sink into your consciousness. Move down to the next line, and again scan from right to left, slowly enough that you can see the shape of each letter.

When you have scanned the final word, speak the words

below the sigil, starting with UB-AH-GEE-TAHTZ.

Say UB-AH-GEE-TAHTZ *three times*, before moving to the next line. Speak the next line three times, and continue like this until you have spoken the final line, SHUH-KAHV-TZUH-YAHT three times.

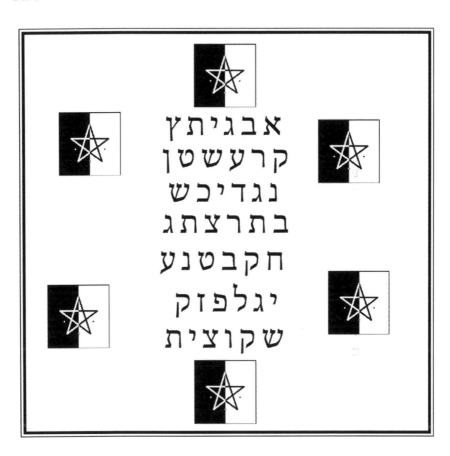

UB-AH-GEE-TAHTZ
KUH-RAH-SUH-TAHN
NUH-GAHD-EE-CHAHSH
BUH-TAHR-TZAH-TAHG
CHUH-KAHB-TAH-NAH
YUH-GAHL-PUH-ZAHK
SHUH-KAHV-TZUH-YAHT

When you have spoken the final line three times, gaze at the sigil below, letting it sink into your consciousness for about a minute. Scan the first line, from right to left, seeing the shape of each letter. Now scan the second line.

When you have scanned all the letters, say this once:

EH-YEAH ASH-AIR EH-YEAH

As written here, this means something like, 'I will become what I please', or 'I will be what I will be'. This is a way of connecting your will, your emotions, and desires to divine power.

Complete the ritual by blessing omnipresent power. You do this by saying the following words once:

BAR-UCH HAH-MAH-KOM

It is done.

The ritual is complete, and you can use the following

rituals now, or at any time in the future.

## The Greater Words of Power

On the following pages, you will find a description of each magickal power, followed by the relevant sigil, with the words to be spoken written below the sigil. Ensure that you have read all the preparatory material, to get the best results.

If you are using a device such as an iPad, and find the device makes it impossible for you to see the sigil on the same page as the words, take the time to write down the spoken words on a piece of paper. This means you can keep the sigil in front of you as you speak the words. On most devices, or in the printed book, this won't be a problem. If you do use a piece of paper, it can be thrown in the trash when you are done.

Take some time to become familiar with the powers, and trust your intuition when it comes to choosing the right ritual for you. And then, most importantly, perform some magick, because it is through the experience of magick that you will understand magickal power.

## Rituals of the Mind

The following eight rituals affect more than just your mind, because they can influence your response to emotions as well, but their focus is primarily on the mental faculties.

## Increase Self Confidence

This magick works to remove the mental and emotional barriers that prevent you from feeling fully confident in yourself. It doesn't boost your confidence artificially, but enables you to connect with your own inner sense of authority, dignity and authenticity. This leads to a rapid increase in self-confidence.

It can be used to increase your confidence in yourself generally, but can also be used to boost your confidence before a difficult time, such as public speaking, being interviewed for a job, or any other situation where you have to put yourself out there.

## Increase Self Confidence

AH-DEER-EAR-AWN
SHUH-GAH-YAH
YEE-KAH-HAH-RAW-VUH-HAH
YEAH-HAW-ELL
RAWG-ZEE-ELL
AHN-PEA-ELL
AH-KAH-NAHV
EH-LAHD

## Complete a Task

Whether you are procrastinating, or simply struggling to find the energy and commitment to complete a task, this magick can work to release you from stagnation.

Use the magick to create a strong sense of commitment to your task, so that returning to it becomes easy. Procrastination is often caused by a fear of commitment to a task, so this magick works by ensuring you feel a deep sense of commitment to the task. It also works by building your sense of pleasure and accomplishment when you work on the task, to make working on it more enjoyable.

This magick applies to any task that requires your time and commitment, whether it's buying a new house or writing your novel.

It can also be used when you have a personal goal that requires commitment. If you've set yourself the goal of running five kilometers, or doing one hundred pushups every day, this magick can help give you the commitment to reach that goal.

## Complete a Task

AH-RAH-REE-TAH
NUH-TAHN-YAH
YEE-SHOO-HAH-KAWV-VAH-HAH
HAW-ELL
SAHN-BEE-ELL
KAHR-ME-ELL
AHT-NAKE
KEH-LEE

## Increase Energy Levels

There can be times when, even if you're looking after yourself and allowing enough time for sleep, your energy levels are low. This magick can unlock your inner energy.

It is also effective when you are feeling close to burnout, and need a renewed sense of vigor.

As with all the magick in this book, it only needs to be used once at any given time in your life. Using it every day will not give you more energy. If, however, something in your life changes, and you lose energy as a result, the ritual should be repeated to account for the new circumstances.

## Increase Energy Levels

ELL-AH-DOE-NIGH
TAHM-TAIL-YAH
AH-YAH-DAW-TAWN-AHTZ-EE-YEE
TOO-VEE-ELL
AH-HAH-VEE-ELL
ME-VAH

## Pass an Exam

You can use this magick right before an exam, but for the best results the magick should be used during the learning period, long before you take the exam. That will ensure that you learn efficiently and recall what you have learnt with ease. This is not a substitute for putting in the time and effort of learning effectively. If used at the last minute, it will assist you, but you are much more likely to get good results if you use it from the outset.

If you're taking a one-off exam, such as a driving test, you should perform the ritual when you first start taking driving lessons (or as soon as you get this book, if your lessons have already started). There is no need to repeat it on the day of the test, but you may want to see the next chapter for a useful exam-day ritual.

If you're studying long-term, and taking many exams, the process is slightly different. You should perform the ritual at the time that you begin your studies (or as soon as you get this book), and then perform it again as soon as the date is set for a particular exam. By aiming this at your studies in general, just once, you give great power to all your learning. By then directing it at each individual exam, well in advance, you enable the best preparation for each exam.

What if you're only given a day's notice before the exam? It is still worth performing this ritual, as it can help you to access your previous learning.

What if it's an exam that tests general competence, physical ability or aptitude? Again, perform the ritual as soon as you know that you will definitely be taking the exam.

**Pass an Exam**

AH-DOE-NIGH
RAHM-YAH
YEE-AH-HAH-VEEV-GEH-HAH
SAH-NAY-GORE
TZEM-EAR-AWCH-DAH
SAHN-SEE-ELL
AHT-NAKE
EH-LEM

## Mental Focus

When you need clear thought for a short period of time, call on this magick. It is ideal for the day you take an exam, or any time when you have to remain focused.

If you are taking a series of tests, over several days, use this ritual each day, as these tests should be thought of as separate events, and the magick works in the short-term.

It can also be used in non-test situations where strong mental focus is required. If you're completing an essay, book or painting, this can give you the required concentration. It can be used by people in sports, on the day of a game.

When you feel the need for mental focus, be assured that this magick can help you obtain clear thought, without excessive fatigue.

## Mental Focus

ACH-AH-TREE-ELL
KUH-MAHL-YAH
YEE-SAH-HAH-TAHV-UN-HAH
TAHF-TAHF-YAH
TZOO-REE-ELL
HAH-REE

## Obtain Peaceful Sleep and Dreams

When you're experiencing a period of troubled sleep, or frequent nightmares, this magick can bring peace to your nights.

You can use this magick at any time during the day, or right before sleep. The ritual only needs to be performed once during any period of troubled sleep, and can break you out of restlessness for a considerable time.

Do not feel the need to repeat it every night before bed. Know that the magick has worked, even though you've only performed the ritual once.

If you ever find that you enter a new period of poor sleep, you can repeat the ritual.

## Obtain Peaceful Sleep and Dreams

EH-YEAH
YEEG-BAH-YAH
AH-YAH-DAW-TAWN-AHTZ-EE-YEE
TAHM-TAHM-ELL
AHZ-REE-ELL
RAH-AH

## Overcome Bad Habits

This magick can help you overcome bad habits by improving your awareness of the habit, your willpower, and your commitment to overcoming the habit. It also works to ease the underlying pain or discomfort that makes the habit desirable to you.

There is no magick that can make you give up an embedded habit, without you putting in tremendous effort of your own. But you are probably already quite used to putting tremendous effort into breaking a habit. When people have habits, they try to break them, and a lot of the time, they fail. If you try again, with full commitment, and with this magick supporting you, you are far more likely to succeed.

Perform the ritual once, and know that you are now able to quit your habit. You may find that the emotional transmutation that takes place in this ritual – where you feel such relief at being free of the habit - can be quite intense.

If you slip up, and lapse back into your habit, there is no need to repeat the ritual. Simply get back on track. Only repeat the ritual if you completely give up on your efforts.

You should also know that for some people, this magick is so potent that giving up a habit is relatively easy. Don't expect this, because as I say above, it's far more likely that you will need to work hard. But if you are one of the lucky ones, and do find that your habit goes effortlessly, enjoy the ease with which you have been released.

## Overcome Bad Habits

ELL-AH-DOE-NIGH
YUH-AH-LEE-YAH
YEEF-HAHZ-VUH-KAY-HAH
AHZ-BOO-GAH
BAH-GEE-AHN
LAH-SEE-ELL
CAH-HET

## Increase Willpower to Eat Well

There is no magick that can make you lose weight, but you can use magick to support your positive eating habits. This can be much more effective than trying diet after diet. You probably already know what you should eat, what you should avoid, and when you are satisfied. All you need is the resolve to eat healthily.

This magick works in several ways, using improved willpower and perception. Primarily, it gives you the willpower you need to make dietary changes that can be uncomfortable at first. Your willpower is supported by an increased awareness of what you consume. Eating becomes an almost sacred time, where you pay calm attention to taste and texture. Your increased willpower enables you to eat more slowly. The magick gives you the awareness and willpower to stop eating when you first sense satisfaction, rather than continuing to eat until overfull.

Perform this ritual once, and it will support you until new habits are fully embedded. It only needs repeating if you find that you slip back into poor eating habits.

## Increase Willpower to Eat Well

TZ-URR-TAHK
NUH-TAHN-YAH
YEE-SHOO-HAH-KAWV-VAH-HAH
HAW-ELL
BUH-DAHF-TEE-ELL
DAH-NOO-ELL
AH-KAH-NAHV
HEH-ZEE

## Rituals That Affect Others

All the magick you perform has an effect on other people, directly or indirectly. The next six rituals have a direct effect on others. If you are uncomfortable using influence magick, then skip this section. But know that these rituals are not used to dominate or control people. They are used to influence people to act in a way that provides your life with more balance.

I consider these rituals to be acts of kindness, because they can render many stressful situations calm, and that benefits more than just yourself. It is also true that the ritual to *Give Comfort to Another* is magick of pure generosity, but you will also obtain a great sense of comfort and reward when it works.

## Stop an Argument Quickly

When an argument is getting out of hand, either in terms of duration or intensity, this ritual can bring peace. This doesn't mean you will get your way or subdue the other party, but it encourages hostilities to come to an end.

You can use this magick when there is a long-term argument, or something that has just come up. It works to reduce enmity within groups, as well as between individuals.

This magick is not aimed at removing the underlying cause of the argument, and does not mean an agreement will necessarily be reached. Its purpose is to put a halt to spite, resentment or anger, before it gets too extreme or hurtful.

## Stop an Argument Quickly

AH-DEER-EAR-AWN
YUH-AH-LEE-YAH
YEECH-EH-HAH-KEV-VAH-HAH
TAHM-TAHM-ELL
HAH-VEE-ELL
SAHF-SAHF-EAR-AWN
REE-YEE

## Receive a Fair Legal Decision

This magick can bring fairmindedness to a legal decision. When it looks like there will be a lack of justice, this magick can help your case be heard clearly and without legal tricks catching you out.

Whether you are wrangling over the details of a divorce, or being accused of a crime, the effect of the magick is to ensure that falsehoods and deception are removed, so that a truly fair decision can be made. It ensures that all parties involved see the truth.

Use this magick with caution. If you are guilty, know that the decision that's handed down will be objectively fair. This doesn't give you the ability to shirk the law. Use the magick only if you feel that you are absolutely in the right, and that you are willing to live with a fair decision.

## Receive a Fair Legal Decision

TZ-URR-TAHK
TAHM-TAIL-YAH
YEE-SAH-HAH-TAHV-UN-HAH
MET-AH-TRAWN
TZOO-REE-ELL
KAHF-REE-ELL
MAH-CHEE

## Subdue Unwanted Attention

Unwanted attention can be extremely unpleasant, but it can be tackled with magick. This ritual can break the fascination, so that the unwanted person loses interest in you.

This magick works when there is somebody in your life who bothers you with persistent unwanted attention. This may come in the form of direct attacks, subtle criticism, undermining or stalking.

If you are being stalked or harassed you should seek the help of the police, but this magick can help to subdue the urges in the other person.

## Subdue Unwanted Attention

AH-RAH-REE-TAH
YEEG-BAH-YAH
YEE-YAH-HAH-GAHV-LEE-HAH
SAH-NAY-GORE
LAH-SEE-ELL
SAHF-SAHF-EAR-AWN
MEB-AH

## Give Comfort to Another

When people you care about are in pain, you can feel extremely helpless. You may offer support and assistance, but sometimes it feels like there is nothing you can do to comfort another. By using this magick, you can convey the warmth of angelic peace onto the one you wish to comfort.

This magick works when the person is suffering from extremely bad news, or when there is ongoing suffering. It does not work to change the actual circumstances, but is a way of offering a level of comfort that can help the other person to recover.

When you perform the ritual, consider your own emotions regarding the other person, and how relieved you will feel when they receive comfort.

## Give Comfort to Another

EH-YEAH
RAHM-YAH
YEE-AH-HAH-VEEV-GEH-HAH
YEAH-HAW-ELL
RAWG-ZEE-ELL
AHR-GAH-MAHN
LAHV

## Make People Warmer Toward You

There are times when you may feel that, in a particular environment, people are not being generous with their affection. There could be a sour atmosphere at work, a coldness within the family, or a withering of affection within a friendship or relationship. Sometimes you may feel that you are generally not as well-liked as you would like to be, and that even strangers are hostile. This magick can help.

If you have a general feeling that you are not being well-liked, or that people are cold, rude or closed-off to you, then you can perform this ritual once, with your focus on that feeling of general social lack. If there is a specific area where you feel the warmth is lacking, focus on that during the ritual, before transmuting the emotion to relief and gratitude.

## Make People Warmer Toward You

AH-DOE-NIGH
KUH-MAHL-YAH
YEE-AH-HAH-VEEV-GEH-HAH
HAH-DAHRN-EE-ELL
SHAHV-REE-ELL
HAIL-AH-ZUH
SEE-AHL

## Encourage Change

This magick is not about coercing somebody to agree with you, but helps the other person to be less fearful, and more outward looking, so that when change is on the horizon, it feels more acceptable.

In business, markets change and the best way to thrive is to adapt. Often, there is somebody within a company who resists change. That might be somebody higher up than you, or somebody who works for you. Whatever the case, this ritual can help the other person be more open to change within a business.

In relationships, it can happen that one person becomes more set in their ways. Sometimes this can provide comfort, but if you are undergoing change, and want to do things, go new places or have a bigger, more open life, this ritual can encourage your partner to be inspired by the change in you.

You may have a friend or family member who exhibits behavior that is unpleasant, illegal or otherwise difficult to live with. This ritual can give them insight and inspiration, to create the desire to change.

The magick is also useful when somebody talks about change, but never actually goes through with it. If you know somebody who openly longs to make a particular change – such as exercising more, taking up a hobby or getting a new job - this ritual can help urge the change to come about.

Focus on *your* feelings during the ritual, not those of the other person. The ritual is about how you will feel when the other person changes, so keep your attention on that.

**Encourage Change**

AH-DEER-EAR-AWN
NUH-TAHN-YAH
YEE-KAH-HAH-RAW-VUH-HAH
HAH-DAHRN-EE-ELL
SAHN-BEE-ELL
SAHN-VEH-REE-ELL
AH-SEE-MORE
HEH-ZEE

## Rituals of Emotion

Human emotions are often described as delicate, but they are powerful forces that can affect many areas of life. By using the magick in the next seven rituals, you can obtain results that are only achievable by working directly on emotion.

## Make New Friends

Although friendship is often regarded as a meeting of minds, with a sense of rapport and agreement, it is always underpinned by an emotional connection. This emotional trust is required for people to see you as a friend. This magick makes people connect with you more readily on that emotional level.

Even if you feel somewhat socially awkward, this magick can help others to see who you really are, making friendship much more likely.

## Make New Friends

ACH-AH-TREE-ELL
SHUH-GAH-YAH
AH-YAH-DAW-TAWN-AHTZ-EE-YEE
TOO-VEE-ELL
DAH-NOO-ELL
SHAHV-REE-ELL
SAHF-SAHF-EAR-AWN
HAH-KEM

## Attract a Romantic Partner

There are entire books devoted to love magick, so what can a simple ritual such as this do for you? It has some limitations, but great potential, and can be applied in two ways.

The first is to encourage a chance meeting with somebody attractive, that you have not met before. If you feel open to the idea of a romantic relationship, perform this ritual, and your chance of meeting somebody you like, and that likes you back, is vastly increased. As with most magick, this doesn't work so well with online meetings. Be prepared to get out in the real world. Also, this ritual does not ensure that a relationship will occur. That is down to you. What this ritual does, is set up chance meetings, where the feelings are enough to set a romance in motion. There is no guarantee that the relationship will be a good one. Again, that is down to you.

The second application of this magick is to open another's heart to you. When you love somebody else, but they have shown no obvious interest in return, this is the magick to use. It's important to note that this magick works with innate emotions, so if there is no attraction at all, it won't work. It can't be used to seduce or coerce somebody against their will, but enables people to drop their guard and truly connect with any attraction they may feel. So if there's somebody you like, and they do not *appear* to like you, be open to this magick. If they have hidden feelings, this magick will help those feelings to emerge. That doesn't mean the other person will declare undying love. You may still be the one who has to make the first move.

## Attract a Romantic Partner

AH-DEER-EAR-AWN
NUH-TAHN-YAH
YEE-NAH-HAH-GEE-VUH-DAH-HAH
TAHF-TAHF-YAH
SHAHV-REE-ELL
KAHF-TZEE-ELL
HAIL-AH-ZUH
YEAH-RET

## End a Relationship Easily

When you want a relationship to end, you need the courage to tell the other person. At the same time, you want to minimize pain. This ritual can give you the courage to state your feelings honestly, without blame, and offers some spiritual and emotional support to yourself and the other person.

Use this only when you genuinely feel that a relationship has run its course. Do not use this to test out your feelings, or see how the other person feels. This magick supports the calm ending of a relationship, when you are certain that the decision is right (even though painful), so it should be used when you really mean it.

Perform the ritual on the day that you intend to end the relationship, and focus on the relief and gratitude you will feel when the relationship ends with peace and friendship.

## End a Relationship Easily

TZ-URR-TAHK
SHUH-GAH-YAH
YEE-YAH-HAH-GAHV-LEE-HAH
AHZ-BOO-GAH
BUH-DAHF-TEE-ELL
YAH-DEE-ELL
SHAHR-SHE-ELL
NET-AH

## Banish Fear and Worry

Without some degree of fear, it would be difficult to function in the world. In many ways, fear keeps us safe. But when fear becomes something that prevents you from enjoying life, that is a problem. I think of worry as habitual fear about things that we cannot change. It is wasted energy, rather than constructive thought. If you feel that fear or worry are tainting your life, this ritual can offer relief.

There are many causes of fear and worry, and if you suffer from anxiety you should seek medical help. But often fear and worry can be induced by underlying emotional issues. This magick helps to calm those emotions, making you far less likely to be bothered by needless fear and worry.

## Banish Fear and Worry

ACH-AH-TREE-ELL
YEE-KAH-HAH-RAW-VUH-HAH
YEAH-HAW-ELL
KAHR-ME-ELL
AHR-GAH-MAHN
NEH-LAHCH

## Improve Your Mood

If you find yourself feeling unusually angry or upset, there can be many causes, from deep seated psychological issues to something as simple as being too tired. This magick cannot solve all those problems, and for any form of depression you will need professional help. But if you find that your mood seems off for no good reason, and that you can't snap out of it no matter how you try, this magick can help. It will not artificially lift your mood, but loosens tangled emotions that could be affecting your spirit.

## Improve Your Mood

AH-RAH-REE-TAH
YEEG-BAH-YAH
YEE-NAH-HAH-GEE-VUH-DAH-HAH
EET-MAWN
BAH-GEE-AHN
AHN-PEA-ELL
AHT-NAKE
AH-NOO

## Improve the Mood of Those Around You

There are times when whole groups of people seem to descend into a bad mood. You may find that an office, family or other group of people becomes more emotionally unsettled than usual, with blame, angst and even anger being prevalent. Being around such groups of people can be very tiresome, so this ritual offers an emotional buffer to the affected group. It will not bring instant happiness, but it eases negative emotions that seem to have infected a group of people.

# Improve the Mood of Those Around You

AH-DEER-EAR-AWN
YUH-AH-LEE-YAH
YEECH-EH-HAH-KEV-VAH-HAH
HAH-DAHRN-EE-ELL
RAWG-ZEE-ELL
HAH-VEE-ELL
AH-REE

## Recover Lost Love

This ritual should be used when you want to rekindle an old relationship. If you still love the person you were once with, this ritual can help the other person to sense your affection for them, and their affection for you. That does not guarantee that your lost love will return, but it does give you the best possible chance at recovering what was lost.

This magick will not make the other person call you out of the blue, so you may need to make contact. Also be aware that if the other person has moved on emotionally, this magick cannot work. But if there is any feeling left, this ritual will help your emotions be communicated, while rousing latent feelings in the other person.

The magick can be used in the immediate aftermath of a breakup, or years later, so long as your feelings are potent, and your desire real.

# Recover Lost Love

אדני
תמתליה
יקהרועה
סניגור
שפניאל
צמרכד
תזדיאל
לכב

AH-DOE-NIGH
TAHM-TAIL-YAH
YEE-KAH-HAH-RAW-VUH-HAH
SAH-NAY-GORE
SHAHF-NEE-ELL
TZEM-EAR-AWCH-DAH
TAHZ-DEE-ELL
LEH-KAHV

## Rituals of Creativity

The next four rituals work on many levels, to remove blockages and encourage inspiration, bring improved creative expression, and an appreciation of your creative work.

## Enhance Creativity

Whether you paint abstracts, write poems, run a business, or work in a marketing department, creativity is an important quality.

This ritual can be used when you need creativity for mundane tasks, such as work, or when you are working in the creative arts. It removes the blockages that prevent you from connecting to your own creative thought processes, and gives you the courage and energy to take mental leaps in new directions.

This magick can be used to enhance your creativity in general, or can be aimed at a specific project - such as a novel or portfolio.

**Enhance Creativity**

EH-YEAH
SHUH-GAH-YAH
YEEF-HAHZ-VUH-KAY-HAH
MET-AH-TRAWN
SAHN-VEH-REE-ELL
PAHK-DEE-ELL
SAHF-SAHF-EAR-AWN
YEAH-ZEL

## Become Popular for Your Creative Work

Creative work feels the most worthwhile when it is appreciated by an audience, and the larger that audience, the greater the pleasure can potentially be.

This is a form of magick that helps other people to see the value in your creative work. You still need to put your work out there, but when you do, there is more chance that it will be noticed and enjoyed.

Let's imagine you've written a novel. You could use this when you're sending the manuscript out to agents and publishers. You could also use it when the book is sent to reviewers, and again when it is released to the public. Whatever field you work in, you can see how easily this ritual can be applied.

## Become Popular for Your Creative Work

ELL-AH-DOE-NIGH
TUH-LAHM-YAH
YEE-SAH-HAH-TAHV-UN-HAH
TAHF-TAHF-YAH
SAHV-TEE-ELL
BEH-HAH-NOO
AH-KAH-NAHV
AWE-MEM

## Improve Visual Skills

This ritual can be used when you need to improve your visual skills. The magick works by helping you to see with more clarity, as well as helping you learn to translate what you see through technique. This applies to any art form that has a visual aspect, from sculpture to photography.

The ritual can be used to increase your skills generally. It can also be used just before you embark on a particular period of training, or when you're trying to learn how to use new equipment or develop fresh techniques.

## Improve Visual Skills

ACH-AH-TREE-ELL
KAH-SEE-YAH
AH-YAH-DAW-TAWN-AHTZ-EE-YEE
TOO-VEE-ELL
KAHF-KEEF-AWE-NELL
YAH-DEE-ELL
CHAH-NEE-ELL
ET-EECH-AH
LEH-LAH

## Improve Musical Abilities

Whether you sing, play an instrument or compose music, this ritual can improve your abilities. It helps you to perceive the structure of music, and increases your ability to apply your skills creatively. The magick can also help you to discover good musical teachers and collaborators.

Used generally, this ritual can bring an improvement to your skills and creative approach. It can also be aimed at a particular project, such as a new song, to help you find new creative depths. Or it can be directed to a particular skill you want to develop, such as learning a new playing technique.

**Improve Musical Abilities**

AH-DOE-NIGH
GAHL-GAHL-YAH
YEE-AH-HAH-VEEV-GEH-HAH
EET-MAWN
SAH-REEL-ELL
SAHN-BEE-ELL
AH-HAH-VEE-ELL
YEAH-YEEL

## Rituals of Transformation

When you perform magick, the outside world changes, but you are also changed. To take this further you can use magick with the intention of achieving a personal transformation.

The final six rituals in this book should be used when you are willing to accept the resulting transformation. This magick will not turn your life upside down, but the transformation can be quite significant, so make sure you want the result you seek through magick.

## The Road Opener

There are times when you feel blocked, stuck, uncertain of the way forward. There are also times when life is going well, but you just need a new direction to be truly fulfilled. At these times, you often feel that you need a breakthrough. You don't just want things to change a little, but you want to find a new direction. This is what *The Road Opener* ritual can do for you.

When you perform this ritual, the emotion is quite abstract, because you do not know, and cannot see, what is ahead of you. When you transmute the feeling of being stuck, it should change to a feeling of elation as you recognize new opportunities. That is the promise of this ritual. It will help you to see new opportunities that could genuinely reward you, on a deep level. It doesn't matter that you don't know what the new opportunities may be. You can imagine how it would be to break free from stagnation, and that feeling will power the ritual.

You can perform this ritual at any time that you're feeling sluggish at work, in relationships, in your creative output or in your general life.

When the magick works you may receive a burst of insight, or see signs that guide you to new opportunities. Sometimes, new opportunities appear out of nowhere, and there's no mistaking them. At other times, the change you seek may occur to you quite gradually. You do not need to actively seek answers, but remain aware of signs, omens and feelings that might guide you in a new direction.

## The Road Opener

ELL-AH-DOE-NIGH
KAH-TAH-KAH-YAH
AH-YAH-DAW-TAWN-AHTZ-EE-YEE
MET-AH-TRAWN
SAHN-DAHL-FAWN
LAH-SEE-ELL
OZ-AH-REE-WHO
AHR-GAH-MAHN
AH-NEE

## Recover Your Passion

This magick helps you recover your passion for an activity that was once dear to you, but that has lost its appeal. It can also be used on relationships that are essentially sound, but lacking in vigor.

If you've lost interest in something, why would you want to recreate that passion? There are times when we lose interest in an activity, and we don't know why. I've known writers, pilots, artists and actors who've lost their passion, and although they could never pin down the exact cause, there seemed to be some doubt, fear or guilt that led to a reduced passion. Getting the passion back can bring tremendous relief.

You don't need to know why your passion faded. Only that you want it back.

This magick can work to help regenerate your interest in your business, your work, in creative pursuits or any activity that you were once passionate about. If you're feeling jaded by something that you have to keep doing, or simply that you have lost interest in something that once mattered to you, this ritual can help you recapture the spark of passion that makes it all feel meaningful and worthwhile.

The ritual works by uncovering your true feelings for something, so it can also be used to put life into a relationship that has lost some of its passion. It will not heal wounds or right wrongs, but it can help you to feel some of the passion you felt in the early stages of a relationship.

**Recover Your Passion**

EH-YEAH
KAH-DAWSH-YAH
YEE-SAH-HAH-TAHV-UN-HAH
YEAH-HAW-ELL
MAH-TAH-MEE-ELL
AH-LEE-ELL
HEH-ZEE

## Overcome Lost Love

When a relationship comes to an end, this ritual can give you comfort, as well as perspective, and a strong sense of self, so that you are able to move on.

Whether or not you are the one that ends the relationship, there can be considerable pain. This magick can help you to recover, without lingering bitterness. It is directed at romantic relationships, but can also ease the pain of a broken friendship.

## Overcome Lost Love

TZ-URR-TAHK
AH-MAH-MAH-YAH
AH-YAH-DAW-TAWN-AHTZ-EE-YEE
SAH-NAY-GORE
KAWCH-VEE-ELL
AH-HAH-VEE-ELL
PAH-HAHL

## Increase Psychic Connection

Do you feel so close to somebody that it feels like you have a psychic connection? Sometimes we can guess what people are thinking, sense their feelings and finish their sentences for them. Often, this is through nothing more than familiarity. Sometimes, though, you may sense a deeper connection. A connection that feels psychic. You can build on that.

If you feel that you have some psychic connection to a loved one, this ritual can make that connection much deeper. Be aware that such connections can leave you more open to being read by the other person, so only use it when there is genuine love and trust.

You can perform this ritual alone, focusing on your connection to the other, or you can both perform the ritual, if you both have an interest in magick. (It can be performed at the same time, or on different days if you prefer).

You will find that in the days and months following this ritual, the connection grows, and you will sense more thoughts, share more dreams, and get a deep intuitive sense of each other's feelings.

If you have little or no sense of a psychic connection, you can use this ritual to encourage one. It may be slight at first, but it can build over time.

## Increase Psychic Connection

AH-RAH-REE-TAH
KAH-SEE-YAH
YEE-AH-HAH-VEEV-GEH-HAH
HAW-ELL
YAW-NEE-ELL
DAH-NOO-ELL
AH-KAH-NAHV
HAH-RAHCH

## Overcome Bitterness, Jealousy and Hatred

When you are trapped in bitterness, it eats away at you. Jealousy makes you exhausted, rather than motivated. Hatred makes you weak, and can amplify an overall sense of sorrow. It's healthy to experience a full range of emotions, because even negative emotions can help you to gain insight into your life. But when you feel stuck in bitterness, jealousy or hatred, turn to this ritual for release.

With this particular ritual, the focus on the negative emotion in the first part of the process can make it challenging to transmute your emotion. The solution is to shift your thoughts to something else altogether; something that generates positive emotions. So you may perform this ritual to get over the jealousy you feel about your brother's thriving career. In the early part of the ritual you focus on that jealous feeling. When it's time to transmute the emotion, it might be too difficult to let go of the jealousy. After all, that's why you're doing the ritual. So forget about your brother, and simply think about *anything* in your life that makes you smile, laugh or feel otherwise happy and relieved. When you capture this emotion, try to add in a sense of gratitude. Feel grateful that your emotions are free once more. At that point, you begin to say the Words of Power. You will find the negative emotions lift after some hours or days.

When adapted (using the instructions from *Adapting the Method*) this ritual can also be used as influence magick, to reduce bitterness, jealousy or hatred in somebody else, making it a powerful way to bring more peace to your life.

**Overcome Bitterness, Jealousy and Hatred**

AH-DEER-EAR-AWN
KAH-TAH-KAH-YAH
YEEF-HAHZ-VUH-KAY-HAH
AHZ-BOO-GAH
SAHN-SEE-NAH-OO-EE
CHAH-NEE-ELL
REH-HAW

## Receive Guidance

An angel cannot tell you what to do, but angels are willing to offer guidance, because they know what it is that you really want. They can sense what you genuinely want, which may be quite different to the things you believe you want. They can also sense which of your desires are most likely to manifest.

By working with this angelic power, you will be able to get past old assumptions and habits of thought, and be guided to know what you really want, and what you can achieve.

You may want a deeper understanding of another person, a situation, or an entire area of your life. There may be an upcoming situation that you don't know how to handle or a decision you have to make. Any time that you wish there was somebody to give you an answer, you can turn to this ritual.

You will rarely hear an angelic whisper telling you what it is that you should do. Most of the time you will get a flash of insight, see a sign or get a strong feeling or intuition about how to proceed. When this occurs, know that you have received the guidance you sought. The magick may be subtle, but it is immensely powerful.

**Receive Guidance**

אהיה
תלמיה
אידתנצי
איטמון
תמליאל
ספספירון
ארגמן
סאל

EH-YEAH
TUH-LAHM-YAH
AH-YAH-DAW-TAWN-AHTZ-EE-YEE
EET-MAWN
TEEM-LAY-ELL
SAHF-SAHF-EAR-AWN
AHR-GAH-MAHN
SEE-AHL

## When Magick Works

The magick in this book works easily for most people, but if you find it difficult, The Gallery of Magick website and blog contains many FAQs, along with advice and practical information that is updated on a regular basis. *The Gallery of Magick* Facebook page will also keep you up to date.

**www.galleryofmagick.com**

If you have an interest in developing your magick further, there are many texts that can assist you. *Words of Power* presents more sigils, using the same method as in this book.

*Magickal Protection* contains rituals that can be directed at specific problems, as well as a daily practice called *The Sword Banishing*, which is one of our most popular and effective rituals.

For those seeking more money, *Magickal Cashbook* uses a ritual to attract small bursts of money out of the blue, and works best when you are not desperate, but when you can approach the magick with a sense of enjoyment and pleasure. For those seeking more money, *Magickal Riches* is comprehensive, with rituals for everything from gambling to sales, with a master ritual to oversee magickal income. For the more ambitious, *Wealth Magick* contains a complex set of rituals for earning money by building a career. For those still trying to find their feet, there is *The Magickal Job Seeker*.

*The 72 Sigils of Power*, by Zanna Blaise, covers Contemplation Magic (for insight and wisdom) and Results Magic (for changing the world around you). Zanna is also the author of *The Angels of Love*, which uses a tasking method with six angels to heal relationships, or to attract a soulmate.

For those who cannot find peace through protection there is *Magickal Attack*, by Gordon Winterfield. Gordon has also written *Demons of Magick*, a comprehensive guide to working safely with demonic power. Dark magick is not to everybody's taste, but this is a highly moral approach that puts the emphasis on using personal sincerity.

*Magickal Seduction* is a text that looks at attracting others by using magick to amplify your attractive qualities, rather than through deception. *Adventures in Sex Magick* is a more specialized text, for those open minded enough to explore this somewhat extreme form of magick.

*The Master Works of Chaos Magick* by Adam Blackthorne is an overview of self-directed and creative magick, which also includes a section covering the Olympic Spirits. *Magickal Servitors* takes another aspect of Chaos Magick and updates it into a modern, workable method.

*The 72 Angels of Magick* is our most comprehensive book of angel magick, and explores hundreds of powers that can be applied by working with these angels. *The Angels of Alchemy* works with 42 angels, to obtain personal transformation.

Our most successful book is *Sigils of Power and Transformation* by Adam Blackthorne, which has brought great results to many people.

**Damon Brand**

**www.galleryofmagick.com**

## Appendix A: What the Words Mean

You can work this magick effectively without ever knowing what the words mean, but I gather that this makes many people feel uncomfortable, so I will make some attempt to explain how this works.

The rituals work by using combinations of divine names and angelic names. These are largely taken from texts such as *Shorshei ha-Shemot*. We have a vast library of ancient texts, and have studied those that we don't own in the great libraries of the world, alongside our own privately inherited collection of materials. The interpretation of these texts revealed the essence of the technique.

Some people ask why Hebrew is used so extensively in magick, and some will answer that it's because Hebrew is an ancient language, others that the Hebrew letters themselves hold divine power, and it can also be said that many of these rituals were devised using Hebrew so they work best when performed in Hebrew. Whatever the truth, you don't need to be able to read Hebrew, because you use the visual scan and the pronunciations I've provided. This makes it work.

The words of the activation ritual are formed by voicing The Forty-Two Letter name of God, which is found in some of the documents mentioned above. There are many debates about the exact vocalization and the one I've included is one that works, which is all that matters

You will notice that the letters in the activation ritual, at one point, are spoken as KUH-RAH-SUH-TAHN. Some people have read this as Kara Satan. When you know that the Hebrew word Kara is 'to bow down' then it looks like you are being told to bow down to Satan, which would be alarming. But this misreading of the words only happens if you work with English approximations. Remember that the sigil is actually written in Hebrew. When you look at the actual Hebrew letters in the sigil, everything becomes clear. I'll assume you can't read Hebrew, but suffice it to say that the letters of the Hebrew word Kara (to bow down) are Kaph, Resh, Ayin. Those are *not* the letters in the sigil. The sigil letters are Qoph, Resh, Ayin, and these make the word Qara, which means 'to tear'.

Even if you can't read any Hebrew you can visit these links, and you will see the second line of our sigil most definitely contains the phrase 'to tear'.

Kara, 'to bow down':
biblehub.com/hebrew/3766.htm

Qara, as used in our sigil, is 'to tear':
biblehub.com/hebrew/7167.htm

It should now be clear that the sigil does not say that you bow down to Satan, but it says, 'To tear away Satan.' Kabbalists have long held that this part of The Forty-Two Letter Name means that you reject, remove or tear Satan away. The phrase is considered so holy that it is included in many Jewish amulets and chants for healing and protection.

It's all too easy to do a quick search on the internet and rapidly frighten yourself, but with thorough research you can see that the letters used in the activating ritual are derived from The Forty-Too Letter Name of God, and an aspect of that name suggests that you will 'tear away Satan'. By speaking these words, you align yourself with your true will and overcome evil, within and without. This is a safeguard within the magick.

But what does the rest of the activation ritual mean? This is something that remains open to debate, and I can't give a definitive answer, because there isn't one. You could say that it is a vocalization of the Name of God. You may look for meaning in Kabbalistic texts, and find that other meanings are ascribed to sections of the Name. In *Shorshei ha-Shemot* you will find that the name is split into three-letter sections, with various interpretations. So UB-AH-GEE has no actual translation, but is related to removing conflict. TAHTZ is related to healing, and so on. This is why you get no sense out of it if you type the letters into Google Translate. These are not words as such, but strings of letters that have deeper meaning within a magickal context. Here, they work to activate the ritual, by activating *your* connection to this style of sigil.

What of the other words? Some are easier to explain than others. The opening words are always divine names, such as Adiriron or Ehyeh. The final word in each sigil is often a Name of God taken from letters in The Seventy-Two Letter Name of God. In between you will find various angelic names, and some words that are made by combining angelic names with other divine names. There are so many sources, you can imagine that explaining every detail would take an entire book five times as long as this one. All you need to know is that the secret combinations of these holy names and angelic names gives you access to the powers described, if you are willing to put in the sincere emotional work required to get results.

Hopefully I've given you enough information that you can see these are not random words, or inventions, just because they don't appear in the standard angel dictionaries. Those popular angel dictionaries often miss out the content of more hidden texts.

If you have an academic interest in this, you can buy a lot of expensive books and it can be fascinating. But if you want to learn about magick, *do the magick*, make room for it in your life and see the power it can bring you. Through experience you discover truth.

**Damon Brand**

www.galleryofmagick.com

Printed in Germany
by Amazon Distribution
GmbH, Leipzig